Illustrations credits:

Archivio White Star/Marcello Bertinetti:
Cover, 2-3, 4, 7, 15, 16, 20, 25, 27, 32-33, 40-41, 48, 52, 60-61, 63, 67, 70, 74-75, 79, 80-81, 91, 92, 94-95

Archivio White Star/Carlo De Fabianis:
10, 18, 26, 28, 34, 38-39, 43, 44, 51, 55, 64, 65, 66, 73, 77, 82, 86.

Archivio White Star/Angela White Bertinetti:
6, 19, 21, 24, 30, 36, 37, 42, 46, 47, 49, 50, 54-56, 57, 62, 68, 71, 72, 76, 93.

A. Bardi/Panda Photo:
31.

A. Board/Panda Photo:
78.

Giuliano Colliva:
Back-cover, 12-13, 22-23, 87, 90.

Comstock/Zefa:
17.

Cesare Gerolimetto:
8, 9, 29, 35, 53, 84-85, 88, 89.

Peria/Zefa:
58-59

Tony Stone/Franca Speranza:
11.

Kohlhas/Zefa:
14.

First published in English in 1991 by Tiger Books International PLC, London.

This 1991 edition published by Crescent Books, distributed by Outlet Book Company, Inc.
A Random House Company
225 Park Avenue South
New York
New York 10003

ISBN 0-517-05876-6
87654321

Printed and bound in Singapore.

INSIDE
NEW YORK

TEXT
PAOLO FONTANA

DESIGN
PATRIZIA BALOCCO

CRESCENT BOOKS
New York

*I*s there anything left to say about New York?

Certainly, the secrets of Manhattan seem to have been almost completely revealed by numerous guide-books, thousands of feature articles and hundreds of stories related by those who live there. Yet those who know New York well claim that there is no other city in the world which is changing so rapidly. Such changes are not limited to places to visit such as restaurants and shops: the way of life in the city is also changing. To give just one example, a guide-book published a few years ago would never have mentioned the lower part of Harlem, the eastern part of the Village or the neighborhood near Colombia University as places to visit. And who could ever have imagined that luxury shops, boutiques and antique dealers would have abandoned their traditional sites in Fifth, Madison or Park Avenue to move elsewhere?

Today, even the most casual visitor quickly becomes aware that in New York, constant change is a way of life.

Certainly, New York is not only Manhattan, and this is something which is all too often forgotten. The tour organizers forget it and probably many New Yorkers have never been to Coney Island or Long Island. But the real "explorers" of this city prefer places which are less traditional and less well-known by foreigners.

Twenty minutes by ferry takes one to Staten Island, for example, where one can dine overlooking the sea and enjoying one of the most fascinating views in the world. The other outer boroughs of New York – Brooklyn, Queens and the Bronx – can all be glimpsed from a Circle Line cruise around Manhattan. Yet, New York City is still a place to live and to enjoy to the full,

even though one realizes, right from the start, that one can never really get to know and understand it. There are too many realities, too many different situations for one to adapt to. New York is continually changing and her inhabitants are constantly searching anxiously for something or someone.

One piece of advice could, however, be given and that is to try to discover the city on foot. Walking can be tiring, but public transport and taxis can rescue the footsore. Every visitor finds his own way of tracking down his own version of New York.

"The present is so important in New York that one tends to forget the past", wrote John Jay Chapman as far back as 1909, and it might therefore not be superfluous to steal a glance at the history of a place which, for each of us, has always represented the future.

The first men who fought for that land which was to become the state of New York were North American Indians. Some Algonquin tribes lived on Long Island and in the southern valleys of the Hudson. The Algonquin people were soon overcome by war-mongering Iroquois tribes under the leadership of their great chief Hiawatha who established an advanced culture in New York state. The Iroquois nations had just finished organizing a system of social order when the whites arrived.

In 1524 Giovanni da Verazzano first set eyes on what was to become New York. It was a fleeting visit and a storm forced the Italian navigator to move out to sea again. Almost a century went by before another explorer crossed the strait which leads from Lower Hudson Bay to present-day Manhattan. With a crew of 18, Henry Hudson re-discovered Manhattan Island and

8 The Trump Tower houses luxury apartments and a shopping center, paneled in pink marble; a cascade of water flows down one wall.

the river that was named after him. He took possession in the name of Holland. A few years later, in 1624, Peter Minuit bought the tip of the island of Manhattan from the Iroquois on behalf of the Dutch West India Company. The cost of this barter was goods worth sixty guilders. The colonization of the territory began with the foundation of the first commercial center, New Amsterdam.

Very soon, New Amsterdam became a disorderly shanty town where pigs, dogs, cats and colonists live in the most absolute propinquity in squalid, unhealthy hovels. It was the iron will of Peter Stuyvesent, the Dutch director-general, that disciplined the young and disorderly colony. By 1660, the majority of Manhattan's 17 streets were paved with flagstones but Stuyvesent's efforts didn't manage to stop the colony from going bankrupt. Following conflict between Dutch and English colonists, four warships, sent out from England, occupied the area and renamed the city after the Duke of York without a shot being fired.

The city remained English until the American Revolution.

In September 1783, the English recognized the independence of the United States. Three months later, they also left New York, while the 'stars and stripes' was saluted by George Washington on the Battery, the southernmost point of Manhattan.

By 1790, New York was the most populous city in the United States with more than 33,000 inhabitants. The first half of the century witnessed a massive expansion of urban centers. This was caused by a number of different factors but was principally due to the large contingents of Europeans who immigrated in

9 The Chrysler Building is one of the city's most glorious symbols. In perfect art deco style, it was completed in 1930. The summit of this building was the setting for the final scenes of the legendary film "King Kong".

this period and to the opening of important communication channels towards the interior of the continent.

In 1825, the Erie Canal was opened to traffic, putting New York in direct communication with the region of the Great Lakes, while, in 1832, the first railroad, the New York and Harlem Railroad, was inaugurated.

The impressive increase in the population was principally due to the immigration of large numbers of Germans and Irish which began before the Civil War. These were joined by Italians, Poles, Greeks, Hungarians, Scandinavians and Russians towards the end of the century. The industrialization of the city encouraged this migratory flow even more. Between 1892 and 1925 more than 12 million immigrants passed in front of the omnipresent symbol of this "open-arms policy", the Statue of Liberty, donated to New York by France.

In 1900 the city was home to 70% of the most important commercial companies in the country. Two-thirds of imports and 40% of all exports passed through the port warehouses of New York. During the first year of the century it hosted the first motor car exhibition to take place in the United States, and work began on the subway system.

Sites on which to build were very expensive and were increasingly smaller, and so the conquest of the sky began. Amid much controversy, the 21-floor Flatiron building was built in 1902. When it opened, it was the tallest building in the world. The history and the future of the city which was to become the "capital of the world" was beginning, and the "skyscraper" was to become one of its most enduring symbols.

14 *A night view of Manhattan from the Empire State Building.*

15 *The Lincoln Center of Performing Arts is the home of New York City Ballet and the New York City Opera.*

17 The Statue of Liberty, omnipresent symbol of American democracy, was sculpted by the Frenchman, Frederic Auguste Bartholdi and presented to New York by France. Its official name is "Liberty which illuminates the world."

18 In the heart of Midtown we find the famous Fifth Avenue. It is considered the most elegant street in New York and marks the natural dividing line between the East and West of the metropolis.

19 left The unmistakable profile of the Citycorp Center stands out in the surrounding grayness of the atmosphere.

19 right The Empire State Building, with 120 floors, was completed in 1931 and was the first "gigantic" skyscraper in the city.

20 left The Helmsley Building dominates Park Avenue.

20 right Avenue of the Americas is one of the city's main roads, with continuous traffic.

21 The facade of the Helmsley building is embellished with a gilded clock in art deco style which contrasts pleasantly with the futuristic lines of the skyscrapers in Park Avenue.

22-23 Although traffic in New York is very intense, it is relatively fast-flowing, because of the rational way in which the city was planned and built.

*T*o know and understand New York thoroughly is a mammoth, impossible task. To have some chance of success, one needs to approach it with curiosity and respect. One can visit New York ten or fifteen times and it will always seem different because this mirage, the incarnation of many aspects of American life and the American dream is really the place of "everyman": everyone can find there what he wants, even what he fears, or simply that which he finds hard to describe in his own dreams. In New York everybody looks for and finds everything. The Italian who is homesick for an atmosphere which no longer exists will find corners, smells and tastes which the urbanized Italian South has forgotten, while the Russian initiated into Gorbachev's reforms can plunge once more into an orthodox religion which has been buried under decades of militant atheism.

Since the first image – the most vivid and striking one – is always the one which gets stuck in the folds of the memory, everyone will have their own personal image of New York. In this way, the outpouring of glass and concrete which rises up before our eyes to form the New York skyline appears both familiar and intimidating. Once we cross one of the many bridges which link the "world" to Manhattan, the shock wave hits us. A subtle yet powerful sensation of having arrived in a universe where time moves in a different way, where the electric quality of life launches thousands of challenges and messages seizes us. Suggestions, slogans, invitations of all sorts follow each other frantically and one must decide what to do first.

26 Since the early years of this century, Fifth Avenue has been a residential neighborhood.

27 A show "on the road" in the best American tradition. When wandering around the streets of New York it's easy to bump into dozens of street artists who are trying to make ends meet while waiting for the big break.

28 The Statue of Liberty is linked to Battery Park in the south of Manhattan by numerous ferries which go backwards and forwards at all hours of the day.

29 A view of the city from Ellis Island, which was the entrance point for more than half the immigrants who came to the United States between 1892 and 1924.

From an architectural point of view, New York cannot be ignored. The post-modern monuments are not to be missed: the famous AT&T block at Madison Avenue and 55th Street and, even more, the so-called "Lipstick", three pink granite buildings each 35 floors high at the crossroads of 3rd Avenue and 53rd Street, are in sharp contrast to traditional building concepts. More reassuring is the IBM skyscraper rendered sumptuous by a large foyer and atrium surrounded by glass walls. Moving downtown, towards the southern part of Manhattan and, in particular, in that area along the banks of the Hudson River, one can observe the "pioneer spirit" in action. Taking shape there is the spirit which animates this city. Neglected, run-down neighborhoods suddenly become the scene of daring projects. An example of these new efforts to interpret reality and change is the Jacob Javits Convention Center which rises up between the 34th and the 38th Streets. It is a triumph of crystal panels which manage to capture every flicker of natural light and this gives the whole building an incredible luminosity.

In the same area, the square towers of the World Financial Center soar sky-wards, linked to each other by a system of public spaces, gardens, glass walls, and little squares with benches and small lamps. New York, however, reveals not only the architect's response to new technologies. Restoration work is being done on relics of fin du siècle architecture, beaux-arts monuments and the Public Library, a splendid building constructed in 1911 to satisfy the intellectual curiosity of anyone who is prepared to search through filing cabinets which list

more than three-and-a-half million volumes.

There is also space for Italian-style architecture and the Italian presence makes itself known in the new Banca Commerciale offices which are characterized by subtle details carved in the external stone facing and in Trump Tower on 5th Avenue, where the Milanese architect Carlo Boeri has designed an apartment rich in works of art with an outstanding view over Central Park. In this relentlessly advancing, futuristic city, some historical oases have still manage to survive and preserve that melting-pot character which for years was thought of as being the very nature of the USA: a mixture of races, languages, religions and nationalities which preserve, in a more accentuated manner than in their respective countries of origin, their national characteristics and their cultural roots, sublimated in their intense pride of being an American and, above all, a New Yorker. In New York it is still possible to immerse oneself in the atmosphere of the popular feasts in Little Italy and taste Sicilian cannoli in cake shops whose art nouveau and rococo style were typical of Turin at the end of the last century.

One can still make purchases in the strict Kosher butchers' shops around Hester Street and taste tea served from magnificent samovars which could have served tea to Russian nobles who fled their country after the October Revolution before finding a home in cafés where the atmosphere of old, holy Russia wafts over the icons hanging on the walls.

Other images are more similar to the picture created by the cinema. The sad and tough streets of the Bowery and 8th

Avenue are peopled with weary and down-trodden figures at any moment of the day and night. These are the streets of misery and drama so similar to those seen in many TV serials, and to find oneself in the midst of them can be a rude awakening.

In the humid and often rainy climate of the metropolis even the sky, reflected in the wide glass-fronted surfaces, takes on different nuances; along the sidewalks and at the sides of the roads, little artificial geysers spurt up, puffs of thick, whitish steam that render the city-scape even stranger; the ground underfoot shudders at the passage of subway trains which accompany the commuters in their ever constant rhythm of work.

30 A helmeted cyclist faces up to the dangers of New York traffic.

31 The Rockefeller Center is a real city within the city. At the center of the entire complex is a sunken square known as "Lower Plaza". In the winter months it is transformed into an ice-rink, while in summer it is a welcoming open-air cafe.

1270 Avenue of the Americas

1270

35 The United Nations Buildings complex consists of four buildings designed by W. Harrison and M. Abramovita. Numerous architects from various nations also collaborated in their construction including Le Corbusier and Niemeyer. The surrounding spaces are adorned with numerous sculptures donated by UN member states.

36 The World Trade Center was built between 1962 and 1977 and has 110 floors. In the background Brooklyn and Manhattan Bridges can be seen.

37 The windows of the skyscrapers create a particular play of mirrors; here, the Plaza Hotel is reflected in the windows of Hugh Hefner's Playboy Club on 59th Avenue.

38-39 On the streets of Manhattan, people walk at a frenetic, almost unified, pace; only tourists are granted the privilege of loitering and admiring shop windows and buildings.

40-41 One of the most elegant and prestigious hotels in New York is the Waldorf-Astoria which was built by William Waldorf on Park Avenue. The ground-floor foyer, in art deco style, is open to the public.

Setting out to discover New York means going into the neighborhoods: Little Italy, increasingly threatened by the expansion of Chinatown; SoHo – 20 blocks whose buildings are faced with an alloy of carbon, iron and silicon which creates the so-called cast-iron effect and where people still walk at night. South-west of SoHo is another New York miracle – TriBeCa. This provides one of the best examples of "gentrification", the phenomenon by which a neighborhood or group of blocks is transformed by the influx of new, emerging classes. The residential area expands and invades areas which were traditionally industrial zones, transforming disreputable areas. Today, the Triangle Below Canal enjoys maximum popularity and like everything in this chameleon-like city, could lose favor overnight. In New York, when someone or something reaches perfection and maturity, it must change, move on.

Even the immense green lung of Central Park, sandwiched between rows of skyscrapers and clouds of smog, becomes a challenge to the commonplace. It is a coin showing the two sides of metropolitan reality. By day, it gaily plays host to frolicsome children, jogging enthusiasts and the chess games of senior citizens. By night, it becomes an appointment with ambush, a surreal theater in which knife-wielding gangs confront each other, while other gangs race up and down the paths on roller skates, their faces distorted by make-up. There are many different ways in which a law-abiding New Yorker can spend an evening. Some choose austere, smoke-filled jazz clubs; some discotheques for teenages like Danceteria, a building where they dance rock-and-roll; some exclusive clubs

in the art galleries; some packed country-and-western style bars; some video-clubs or art and drama clubs where one is scarcely able to distinguish either the art or the drama. The professional night-birds go to Brazilian bars where it is always carnival, or else they go to Limelight, situated in a beautiful old deconsecrated church. Other possibilities are Roxy, the home of break-dancing or one of the countless piano bars.

Those who like jazz can still seek refuge in the Village Vanguard, a small club where Mingus, Coltraine and Thelonius Monk all played; and finally, the real, true, unique Cotton Club of Harlem. At the moment, the "in" places are a fistful of rock discos in the city center, multi-media places where almost theatrical-type shows follow one another without interruption. The Area, for example, is transformed continuously with every nuance in fashion. Another mecca of entertainment is the Palladium on East 14th Street – a New Wave experiment created in an old theater by the Japanese architect Arata Isozaki. The place is full of works by contemporary artists and the vouchers for the drinks were designed by none other than Andy Warhol.

It is not easy to get into these clubs. The all have a computerized list divided into categories of client and each of them works on the basis of invitation-only evenings. Yet, even for those with an invitation it is not easy to get in. One must first pass the feared and final judgment of the doorman. If he is in a bad mood and if you look too anonymous there is nothing to be done. If he's in a diplomatic mood, he will tell you that the club is full: there is no point in insisting.

44 *Grand Central Station is one of the two main railroad stations in New York. In this picture, we can make out the clock surmounted by a neo-classical sculpture by Jules Coutan.*

45 *Interior of Trump Tower: on the ground floor, in a strange and very American mix of business and religion, we find St. Peter's Church.*

46 The Guggenheim Museum houses changing exhibitions of modern art as well as a large permanent collection of modern works. It was founded by Solomon Guggenheim, a travelling salesman who became an entrepreneur and art collector.

47 The Metropolitan Museum of Art is, without doubt, the most important monument to culture in the Big Apple. In its five blocks there are three million exhibits. Everything is on show here: Joan of Arc's helmet, masterpieces of the Italian Middle Ages and Renaissance, Roman statues and works by Picasso.

48-49 Many New York roof terraces are equipped with swimming pools, tennis courts and mini-golf courses to make up for the lack of time and other open spaces within easy reach.

52 In Central Park you can hire horse-drawn carriages to enjoy the city in an unusual way.

53 top Central Park also contains a lake which is the setting for boat trips and small sailing races. In the center of this body of water, Bow Bridge stands out, a masterpiece in wrought iron, designed by the architect Vaux.

53 bottom In the shaded tranquillity of Central Park, people can devote themselves to sport and other pastimes, forgetting for a few hours that they live in the most frenetic city in the world.

What is the spirit of New York?

Let us stop for a moment and observe the world around us, the interminable to-ing and fro-ing of people: groups of fashionable young people, elderly eccentrics, imperturbable Chinese, smart businesswomen. Every face is charged with personality and security derived from a strong sense of individuality and independence which has been acquired perhaps with great effort.

The New Yorker comes from all corners of the earth and New York is the concrete representation of the Tower of Babel where, however, the people understand each other, or at least make an attempt. From the Korean who sells fruit on the corner of the Bowery to the yuppie of Wall Street, they all have something in common: a taste for life which is viewed as a challenge, the American dream of a promised land which emerges from a sea of adversity.

The feeling of challenge can be sensed in the very eccentricity of the people walking along the sidewalk, and in the streetwise characters who live and struggle to survive in New York. Thus, along with clouds of smog one also breathes tolerance and skepticism in this city, a desire for progress and worldliness, violence and solidarity. It is this pot-pourri which makes New York the liveliest and most enigmatic city in the world. Today, men in skirts, little girls decked out in leather and chains and grannies in hot-pants do not arouse the slightest interest. Non-conformism, creativity and strangeness create an atmosphere that can only be found in the Big Apple.

The craziest and most absurd things acquire added vigor in

Greenwich Village (the Village), Chelsea and Times Square. All the extravagances and follies of this remarkable city find their expression on the night of Hallowe'en. Every year, on the 31st of October, the most unbridled fantasy and even nightmares and fears take shape in a frenzied procession which parades through the narrow streets of the Village. The march is accompanied by chaotic sounds made by everyone who is capable of holding an instrument.

In like manner, the Village and Times Square experience this spirit throughout the rest of the year. In these neighborhoods one finds the same exuberance, the same rowdy way of facing the commonplace. The Village and especially the East Village are prime examples of urban diversity – places of poverty, of bohemian life and of the newly-rich.

Professionals and 'alternative' culture mingle in Astor Place, while aspiring artists and itinerant salesmen try to keep the jaded hippie myth alive. All the alternative fashions, the dreams of many generations, have passed along these streets, from beatniks to punks. Now even here the sidewalks and shops, the streets and the people are being polished up in the eternal pursuit of success and well-being.

For decades the East Village has been the home of Ukrainian, Polish, Hispanic and Italian communities attracted by the atmosphere of tolerance and the low rents. Today, gentrification has struck the tumble-down grocery stores and tenement blocks. Now these old buildings are home to radical chic art galleries, a new market of young artists in search of fame.

58-59 Yankee Stadium, the most important baseball ground in the United States, is host to many eagerly-awaited games.

60-61 A group of young people, relaxing on a bench along Brooklyn Promenade.

62-63 If it seems almost anonymous during the day, Times Square is radically transformed at night when it is illuminated with pulsating neon signs.

64 Radio City Music Hall is the largest covered theater in the world and can seat up to six thousand people.

*I*f New York is a show how can one refuse a walk along Broadway? Broadway is certainly the most famous of the large streets in the city; a dazzling diagonal of neon lights, in the capital of light. It is no coincidence that it has been baptized the "Great White Way". At night, this glittering canyon becomes an almost surreal magical tunnel studded with lights which seem to move as if they had a life of their own. Here, on Broadway, one has yet another sensation of the constantly changing nature of the city: of a restless tempo of life and of an unending stream of visual messages.

The story repeats itself in every street. Every corner of New York is New York and represents its spirit and its characteristics. Broadway is the mecca of great artists: actors, ballet dancers, directors, musicians and producers all strive to get here. In the theaters of this district the most important American and English plays and the most prestigious musicals are performed.

Here we can get to know great old theaters like the Empire, the Apollo and the Liberty. Here you can watch a show at New York's oldest theater, the Lyceum, or plunge into Off-Off Broadway where the most interesting and innovative works of contemporary theater are staged.

Art and drama are everywhere. It might sound like a slick, second-rate slogan: however, this is another of the city's secrets. There is art for the elite and poor art, the dramatic art of everyday life and of every Sunday spent in Central Park.

Let us turn again to this strange green phenomenon which, despite everything, thrives. While many Americans own a well looked-after backyard or a balcony, New Yorkers have Central

65 A show at Radio City: a gilt proscenium similar to the spire on the Chrysler building frames the stage of the music hall.

65 A show at Radio City: a gilt proscenium similar to the spire on the Chrysler building frames the stage of the music hall.

Park, another place which is always in turmoil, peopled by a whole universe of metropolitan types: housewives on anti-stress outings, distinguished businessmen in morning coats and hats, madmen involved in serious arguments and serious people flying off the handle. Despite the enormous crowds which frequent it and the use and abuse to which it has been subjected, the park continues to live and to offer hospitality to everyone. There are little children who cause panic on fast skates and skateboards, jazz musicians and rock bands with their own generator to provide amplification, all sorts of people on soap boxes, gurus of unheard-of religious sects, joggers, drug addicts, petty thieves, and families intent on devouring hot dogs and french fries.

There are many ways of exploring the park: hiring a good mountain bike or a capricious horse, going on foot or on roller skates. For those with no economic problems there is also the snobby and expensive but very romantic horse-drawn coach service.

(The park should be avoided at all costs in the evening when it becomes the jousting ground for the most violent elements who move around in the Big Apple.)

The "Picnic" rite is celebrated every Sunday in Central Park. Families who do not know each other club together and share a meal. To participate in this enjoyable event helps one to understand something of the spirit of the city and its contradictions. As soon as it stops moving, the "Big Apple" becomes more human, almost drowsy, joyful and relaxed, but beware! It only does so because tomorrow is Monday again and

it is necessary to recharge and be recharged, to get ready to return to the business of surviving. The thing which probably causes most amazement about Central Park is the very fact that it exists, with its ingenious layout, its rich and at times exotic greenery and its altogether country-like atmosphere.

Central Park is a breath of fresh air in the midst of metropolitan life, a safety valve and the guarantee that one can continue to live and be happy "despite it all".

No-one better than a New Yorker knows the art of living and of making the best of a daily life which can be problematic.

66-67 Greenwich Village is the mecca of New York non-conformity where madness and creativity often mingle in a strange and fascinating union.

68-69 In the "Village", little street shows are a familiar sight from Sheridan Square to St. Mark's Place. There are also some excellent and unusual shops.

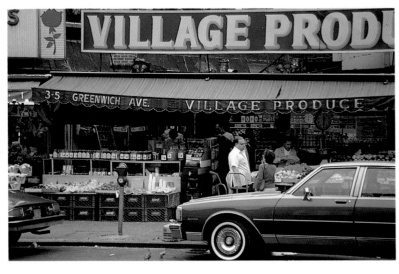

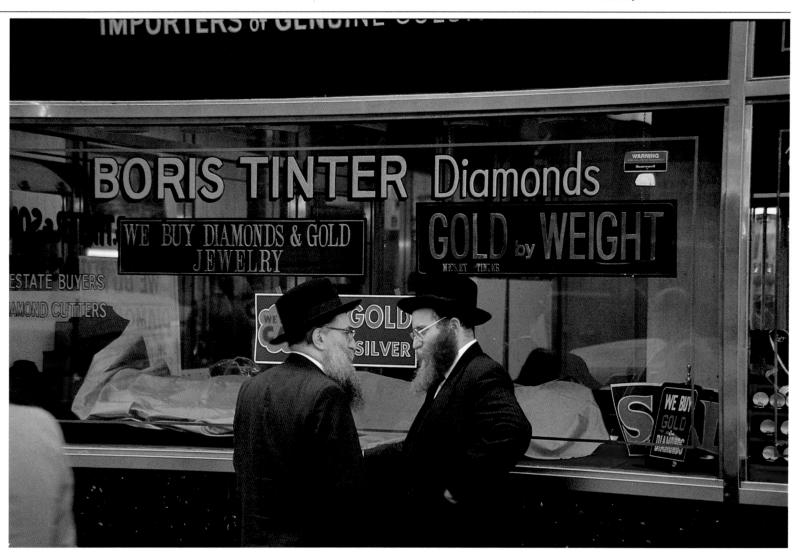

71 In SoHo, many blocks are characterized by picturesque facades made from an alloy of iron and carbon. The picture shows a group of Italian-Americans sitting under the sign of one of the many political associations.

72-73 *Little Italy, the cradle of Italian tradition, is situated to the north of Central Street. The Italian-Americans of the last generation have moved out leaving behind their parents and grandparents, but everyone comes back for the feast of San Gennaro.*

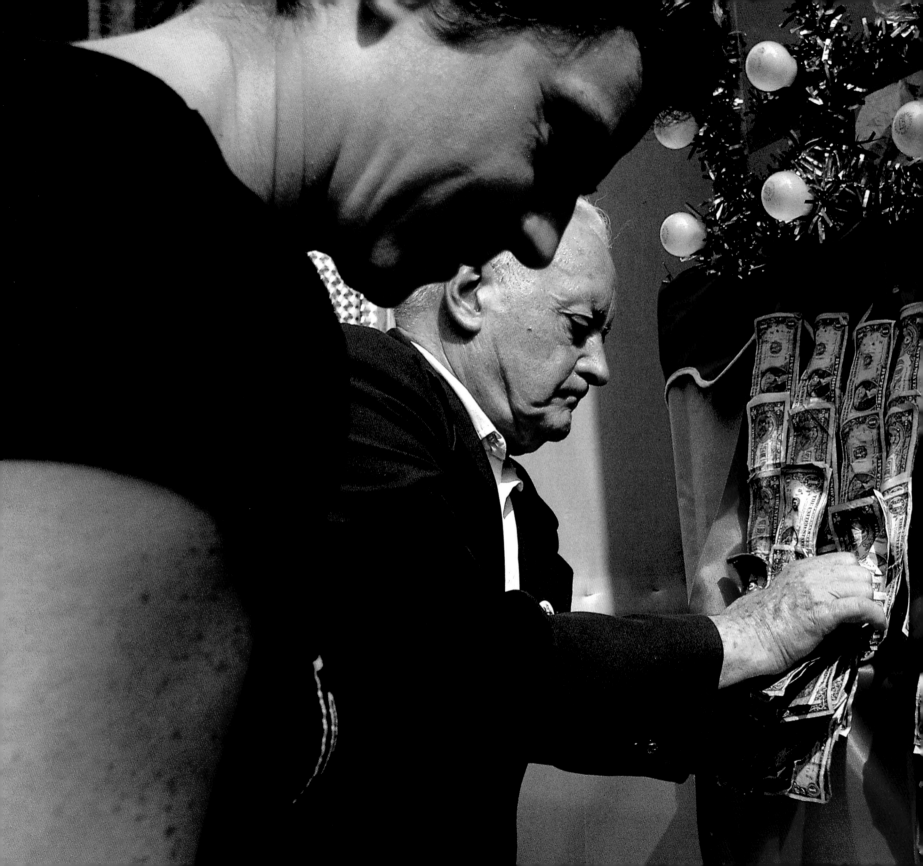

74-75 The feast of San Gennaro is celebrated every year in September. On this occasion Mulberry Street is filled with hundreds of market stalls on which are displayed all the typical Italian products. The event culminates in a procession and the ritual offering to the statue of the patron saint.

76-77 Chinatown is an Asian microcosm where Cantonese dialect and cuisine are no longer the predominant culture. Nowadays, alongside the Chinese, there are people from many other South-East Asian countries.

*I*n New York art is everywhere. One can encounter it simply strolling in the city and looking at the graffiti-daubed walls. In European cities and towns one can admire works of art in museums and then go outside and discover in the streets traces of antiquity dating from the Middle Ages and the Renaissance. Like the rest of America, New York has no past, or better, its past is tied to a very young western civilization which has produced monuments which are, at the most, three hundred years old. This explains the typically American need to venerate the past and also to produce art.

Buildings are disemboweled and demolished, or, at least, restructured. City districts which, a few years ago, were the "paradise of crime" are transformed into fashionable or commercial areas. The very process of changing, and the rapid evolution of lifestyles attracts artists (and those who presume or aspire to be such) who repay the city by making it the major focus of visual and acoustic activities. Even the casual observer will see that art is everywhere: in the improvised artistic shows on the streets, in the graffiti in the subway and in the bright murals which are painted on to walls overnight, in the drawings for sale at street corners and in the itinerant exhibitions in the galleries.

In New York, there is a strong commercial link between art and the rest of the world. The art market in New York surpasses itself each year and the work of artists who are almost unknown in Europe can fetch millions of dollars. There is very rarely calm on the New York art scene: as soon as a particular trend disappears or falls from favor, it is immediately replaced by

78-79 Wall Street is at the center of the Financial District. It takes its name from a wall which the Dutch built to protect the area from the Indians. It is the seat of the New York Stock Exchange, the heart of American financial life.

another new movement.

New York is the place where, if an artist grits his teeth, he can live, study and make a career. Certainly, not all the artists who come here think they will make it, but they try. Once again, this is the way of the American Dream. All those who make a living from art know that they must go to New York to show their works and compare them with the works of the others. Thus, the city boasts an impressive number of museums of an extremely high quality: the Metropolitan Museum of Art is the largest in the world. In its vast rooms one can travel from Prehistory to the Middle Ages via ancient Egypt. The Museum of Modern Art houses important examples of Impressionism, Surrealism, Cubism and Abstract Expressionism. And then the Guggenheim Museum: circular rooms which contain all the more modern masters: Klee, Mirò, Kandinsky, Picasso. Today the new artistic frontier is to be found in the East Village. The Lower East Side has attracted the "nouvelle vague," incongruously mixed with pushers and punks. Here one can explore avant-garde techniques: graffiti and neo-surrealism; new ideas about communication and graphic art, minimalism and neo-pop, new-wave and no-wave prosper here. The entire city provides room for alternative art and events. These alternative galleries offer space to artists who otherwise would have nowhere to exhibit. The alternative becomes the fashion and a commercial business, but this is all part of the game.

80 Brooklyn Port and Lower Manhattan seen from Brooklyn Heights.

81 Navigation on the Hudson River. The river is navigable for 150 miles as far as Albany. It is named after the explorer Henry Hudson.

82 More than 50,000 people work in the World Trade Center and the majority of them come from New Jersey. Every day it is visited by 80,000 people, mostly businessmen.

83 Firemen at work in front of the imposing towers of the World Trade Center. The twin towers reach a height of 1,350 feet.

84-85 Manhattan consists of an island which is surrounded by the Hudson and the East Rivers.

86 The statue of Prometheus, in the Rockefeller Center, has become one of the most well-known symbols of New York.

87 An emblematic image of the Statue of Liberty at sunset. There is an elevator which takes visitors to the top of the pedestal and from here one can climb on foot to the crown, from which one can enjoy incomparable views.

There is a fever that grips everyone who sets foot in New York and tries to extricate himself: a fever to live, produce and buy. Are we, or are we not, in the paradise of consumerism? No other city can boast the same quantity of shops and boutiques as New York. Some of these compete in size and sumptuousness with the museums themselves and, like museums, they bear witness to everyday life, to the importance of the ephemeral, the cult of the image which originates here, and from here is exported to the unsuspecting European capitals which think that they have invented it. Once more, the Big Apple can be seen as a city laboratory where fashions confront each other and prosper. In the course of a fashion parade, the destiny of a fashion designer can be decided. Here you can get lost in enormous luxury department stores such as Bloomingdale's or Macy's. You can visit the splendid shops which have sprung up on Madison Avenue where the well-established shop windows of Armani, Ungaro, Missoni and Versace prosper and where one can also find the latest creations of Kenzo and Tricot.

Naturally, New York offers not only luxury consumption. In the lower part of Broadway, friendly street traders sell their wares to tourists without cheating them. The army and navy stores offer jeans and training-shoes, military and casual clothes at very low prices.

And between one purchase and the next, what about one of those famous quick meals? In no other place in the world can one appreciate the cuisine of the five continents: Turkish kebabs, Sicilian cannoli, Cantonese rice, Sangria, Jewish and Slav specialities. There is an embarrassing array of choices: one can eat at mahogany tables or in smoky drugstores. There are no longer many true drugstores and yet something of the atmosphere of the American provinces can still be felt at Woolworth's and in Lamston's 5 and 10 stores.

Here there are still soft drinks on tap and corners in which to sip long American coffees. Here one can buy the most kitsch souvenirs: Cadillac-lighters, Empire State Buildings with built-in clocks, Statues of Liberty with built-in thermometers and useless and incredible objects of the strangest sort.

To get to know New York means above all being able to get around on foot. The subways are constantly crowded and the buses crawl along in enormous traffic jams. When walking, one is able to observe for oneself that to live here you need strong nerves. One survives by joining up with people who do the same job, have the same ethnic origin, or have had the same fortune or misfortune. New York is a place of unending movement: people are hurled up and down dozens of floors in elevators; there is a constant coming and going, non-stop telephoning, queuing, running to get a place at table, the impression of being in a race. To go there as a visitor is in a certain sense to discover one's future and see the things, both pleasant and unpleasant, which other cities may have to face. It is like taking a leap 20 or 30 years into the future. New York is not a place for relaxed and contemplative tourism: it is necessary to approach it with the desire to learn and discover.

88 *The art nouveau architecture of a building on Fifth Avenue contrasts with the rigid structures of the more modern skyscrapers.*

89 St. Patrick's Cathedral is the largest Catholic church in the United States. Its Gothic-style cusps rise up evocatively among the skyscrapers. In front of the church, one can admire Zac Lawrie's statue of Atlas with the world on his shoulders.

90 The United Nations complex is situated in First Avenue between 41st and 48th Street. The three buildings into which it is divided are characterized by an austere style as if to underline the importance of the institution.

91 The monolithic structure of the twin towers of the World Trade Center make the other sky-scrapers look like toys.

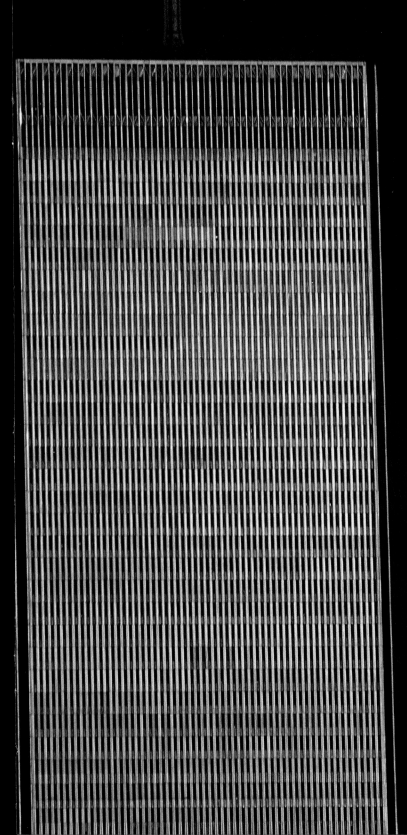

92-93 *An impressive sequence of a hurricane which hangs threateningly over the skyscrapers of Manhattan.*

94-95 *A view of Lower Manhattan at dusk. The skyline is highlighted by the play of light and shadow which create a particularly alluring atmosphere.*